55/1190&91L

HALLELUJAH! What a Savior!

The Crucified and Risen Christ

Music by
Lloyd Larson, Faye López, R. Kevin Boesiger,
Larry Shackley, Molly Ijames, Mark Hayes
and Pepper Choplin

Narration by Pamela Stewart
Orchestrations by Brant Adams, Mark Hayes, Ed Hogan,
Michael Lawrence, Stan Pethel, and Larry Shackley

Editors: Lloyd Larson and Bryan Sharpe
Music Engraving: Jeanette Dotson and Linda Taylor
Cover Design: Ashley Donahue

A Lorenz Company • www.lorenz.com

Foreword

It is an amazing thing to observe the pendulum swing of emotion that scripture indicates transpired in the last days of Jesus' earthly life: from the euphoria surrounding His triumphal entry into Jerusalem on Palm Sunday to the desolation of the lonely Garden as He fully embraced God's plan and ensuing death; from the genuine love conveyed to His faithful followers in the Upper Room to the loneliness experienced in His final hours as those same followers rejected and abandoned Him; from the anger that filled the hearts of those who now called for His crucifixion (only hours after having hailed Him as King) to the tender resignation of a Roman soldier that this indeed was the Son of God; from utter despair as He died on a cross to triumphant joy as Christ's followers began to realize that His prophetic words had become reality - that He had indeed been raised from the dead! All of this, and so much more.....within a single week!

The varied emotions displayed in this remarkable week are not foreign to our own life-experiences as we live this side of eternity. There are seasons of joy and seasons of despair; mountain-top experiences blended with experiences in the "valley of the shadow of death." But ultimately, we shall stand before the living Christ in a climactic celebration of life's journey! We have been extended an invitation to live forever and to worship the King of kings and Lord of lords. Someday all followers of Christ will be able to bow before the Messiah joining in one voice as we proclaim:

Worthy is the Lamb who was slain, to receive power and wealth, and wisdom and strength,
and honor and glory and praise forever and ever! Amen!

Hallelujah! What a Savior!

—Lloyd Larson and Bryan Sharpe, Editors

Contents

Some of the cover-art images and graphics from this work are available as free downloads. We hope that you can use them to assist in the making of your bulletins, posters, flyers, website and email announcements, and in any other way that's within your organization and in conjunction with performances of this work.

To access these files, please visit www.lorenz.com/downloads and navigate to the desired folder. PC users should right click and choose "Save Target As..." and Macintosh users should click and hold the link, then choose "Save Target As..." We have provided standard file formats that should be usable in most page layout or word processing software.

Due to the vast number of differences in computer system setups, we are unable to provide technical support for downloadable images/graphics by either phone or email.

The King Is Coming Today!

Words by **Lloyd Larson**
and **Theodulph of Orleans;**
tr. **John M. Neale**

Music by **Lloyd Larson**
Incorporating **ST. THEODULPH**
by **Melchior Teschner**

1 **Joyously** ♩. = ca. 56 *gradually building in intensity*

Narrator: Crowds lined the streets of Jerusalem,

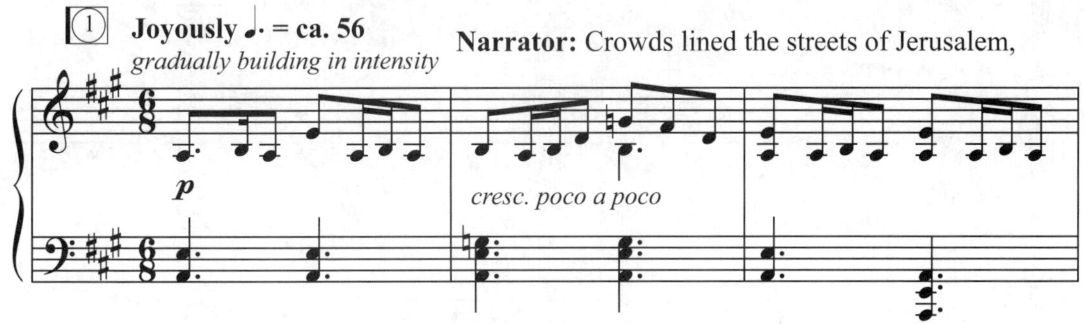

pressing forward, eager to catch a glimpse of Jesus. As He came into view, they praised Him,

as if their very cries could crown Him King!

☐ indicates CD track number.

10
peo - ple shout, "He comes in the name of the Lord!" Praise the
13
King of kings, lift your voice and sing, "He comes in the name of the
2
16
SA
Lord!"
Rocks cry out, the
TB
mel.
Let the rocks cry out, let the

19
peo - ple shout, "He comes in the name of the Lord!"
peo - ple shout, "He comes in the name of the Lord!" Praise the
22
King of kings, your voice and sing, "He comes in the name of the
King of kings, lift your voice and sing, "He comes in the name of the
25
3
mel.
Lord." Ho - san - na, ho -
Lord!"

28
san - na! The King is com - ing to - day! Ho -
31
san - na, ho - san - na! With palms pre - pare Him the -
34
way.
The King is com - ing to -

4

37

day!

40

f

Let the rocks cry out, let the peo - ple shout, "He

43

comes in the name of the Lord!" Praise the King of kings, lift your

46
5
voice and sing, "He comes in the name of the Lord!" All
49
glo - ry, laud, and hon - or to Thee, Re - deem - er,
52
King, to whom the lips of

55
chil - dren made sweet ho - san - nas ring.
58
Thou art the King of Is - ra - el, thou
61
Da - vid's roy - al Son, who in the Lord's name

6
64
com - est, the King and bless - ed One! Ho -
67
san - na, ho - san - na! The King is com-ing to -
70
day! Ho - san - na, ho - san - na! With

73 [7]

palms pre - pare Him the - way. The

76

cresc.

King is com - ing to - day, to

cresc.

cresc.

79

ff

day, to - day!

ff

ff

8vb

Narrator: Many in the crowd were curious. They had heard that Jesus could heal the sick and raise the dead. Others had witnessed these miracles firsthand: wedding guests who celebrated with the water He turned into wine; friends who looked on as He brought Lazarus back to life; lepers who saw the disease vanish from their bodies; and many who sat on a hillside as the Teacher fed thousands with the lunch of one child.

His own disciples had seen Him calm the raging sea with a wave of His hand. Amazed like everyone else, they wondered, "What kind of man is this? Even the winds and the seas obey Him." ***(music begins)***

Lord of the Wind and the Sea

Words by **Lloyd Larson** based on **Matthew 8:27** and **John 3:16**

Music by **Lloyd Larson**

10
Lord of the wind and the sea.
He healed the lame, made the
13
9
blind to see.
16
mp
Je - sus the hum - ble car - pen - ter's Son, re -
mp
mp

18
mf
vealed by God as the Ho - ly One! Ser-vant to all, the
mf
mf
21
10
f
strong and the weak, with truth He comes to those who seek.
f
f
6
24
mf
Lord of the wind and the sea. He
mel. mf
He is the Lord of the wind and the sea. He
mf

27
calmed the storm and He res - cued me.
calmed the storm and He res - cued me. He is the
29
Lord of the wind and the sea. He healed the lame, made the
Lord of the wind and the sea.
32
11
blind to see.
mp
He

35
mp
He raised the dead by God's
turned the wa - ter in - to wine,
mp
38
mf
pow'r di - vine. On the moun - tain-side the crowd was fed with a
mf
mf
41
f
12
few small fish and some loaves of bread.
f
6
f

44
mf
God so loved the world that He
mf
mp
mf
47
gave His on - ly Son, that all who be -
50
13
lieve in Him might be won
to the

53
mp
the Teach - er from Gal - i - lee.
mp
Lord of the wind and the sea,
mp
56
poco rit.
Lord of the wind and the
He is Lord of the wind and the
poco rit.
59
a tempo dim. poco a poco molto rit.
sea.
dim. poco a poco
sea.
a tempo dim. poco a poco molto rit.
p

Narrator: It was now Passover evening. Jesus knew that His time with the disciples was growing short. The One they called "Master" knelt before them like a servant and washed their feet. "Follow my example," He said. "Serve as I serve you now, that the world might know Me through you." Then He stood and, blessing the bread and cup, said, "This is my body; this is my blood. I give them for you. Eat, drink, and remember." ***(music begins)***

Gathered in the Upper Room

Words by
Patricia Mock & Faye López

Music by **Faye López & Patricia Mock**
Inspired by **Gabriel Faure's *Pavane***, Op. 50

10
15
fore He had to go, with ten-der-ness He showed such care.
SA
13
Sit - ting 'round the ta-ble for a meal, He shared with them the Fa - ther's
TB
p
16
mp
will. There, to-geth - er in the Up-per Room, pre -
mp
mp

16
19
p
par - ing now for what would come.
p
8va
p
Poco più mosso ♩ = ca. 80
22
mf
"Peace I leave with you, not as the world would
mp
"My peace I leave with you, not as the world would
Poco più mosso ♩ = ca. 80
mf
25
for -
give, that your joy may be com - plete, for -
mf
give, that your joy may be com - plete, for -

28
ev - er with me
17
live."
rit.
ev - er with me, with me live."
ev - er with me live."
rit.
mp
Tempo I ♩ = 76
31
p
Oo
mp
Then the Mas - terwashed the feet of men, not just His ser - vants, but His
Tempo I ♩ = 76
p
34
mf
"When you take this cup and eat this bread, re -
mf
friends.
mf

18
37
cresc. e accel.
f
mem - ber Me and all I've said.
As I
cresc. e accel.
f
cresc. e accel.
With assurance ♩ = ca. 80
39
love you, love one an - oth - er, as I
With assurance ♩ = ca. 80
f
41
serve you, serve each oth - er, let your

43
light shine! Let the world see a re -
mf
mf
mf
19
love."
45
flec - tion of My love, My love."
mp
mp
love."
mp
cresc.
a tempo
"Peace, my peace I
47
rit.
f
"Peace I
f
rit.
f a tempo

49
mf
leave with you, not as the world would
mf
leave with you, not as the world would
mf

51
give, that your joy_____ may
f
give, that your joy may
f

53
be com - plete,_____ for - ev - er with Me
be com - plete, for - ev - er with Me

20
live."
rit.
Tenderly ♩ = ca. 63
live."
mp
live, with Me live."
Know - ing now the
Tenderly ♩ = ca. 63
rit.
mp
mp molto rit.
p a tempo
gath-ered in the Up - per Room.
mp
p
time was draw-ing near,
8va
molto rit.
p a tempo
rit.
(8va)
rit.
pp
8va
ppp

Narrator: When they had finished the meal, they went to a garden called Gethsemane. There, as Jesus knelt to pray, He agonized over the suffering that lay ahead. In the silent darkness of the night, the Son cried out to His Father: "If there is any other way, please take this cup of death from Me. Nevertheless, Thy will, not mine, be done." ***(music begins)***

Gethsemane Prayer

Words by
R. Kevin Boesiger,
based on **Matthew 26:39**

Music by
R. Kevin Boesiger

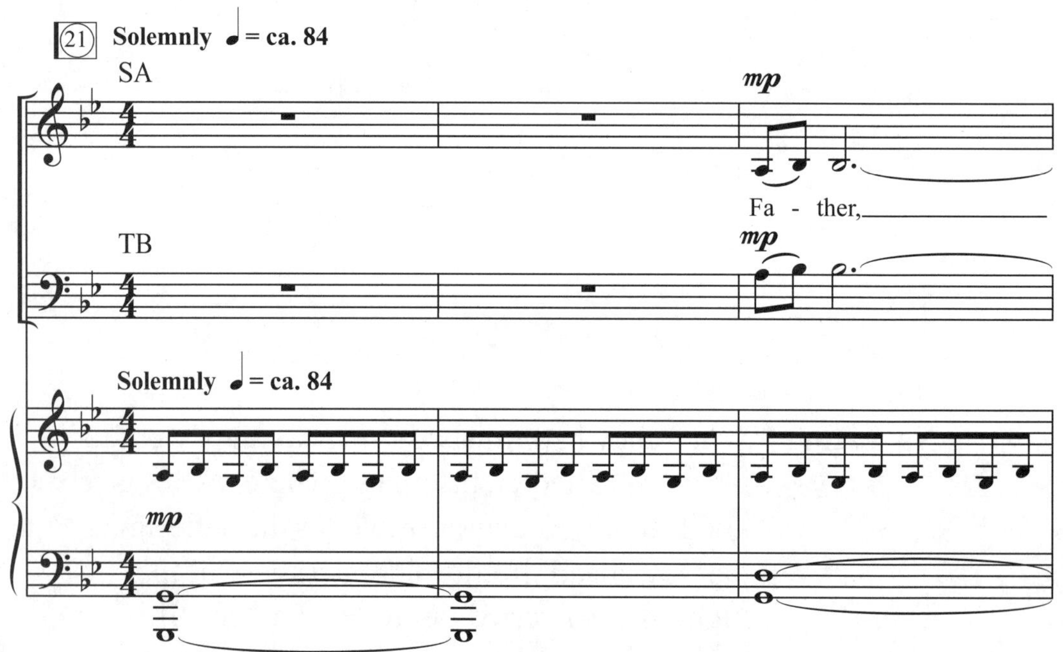

7
let this cup pass o - ver me.
o - ver
10
Fa - ther,
O,
me.
Fa - ther,
13
22
cresc.
take this cup from me.
cresc.
cresc.

16
mf
But not my will, but
mf
But not my will,
mf
19
not my will, not my will but
but not my will,
22
23
Your's be done.
dim.

25
mp
O, my Fa - ther, O, my
mp
Fa - ther, my Fa - ther,
mp
28
Fa - ther, please let this cup pass
31
o - ver me. O, my
o - ver me. Fa - ther,

34
Fa - ther,
please take this cup from
37
24
cresc.
mf
me.
But not my will,
cresc.
mf
But
not my will,
cresc.
mf
40
but not my will,
but not my will,

43
cresc.
not my will but Your's be done.
cresc.
cresc.
46
f
O, not my will,
f
f
49
not my will, but Your

52
dim. e poco rit.
p
will
be
done.
dim. e poco rit.
p
dim. e poco rit.
56
a tempo
p a tempo
59
rit. poco a poco
rit. poco a poco
pp

Narrator: As Jesus finished praying, the silence in the garden was broken. Led by Judas, a group of men armed with swords and clubs arrested Jesus and brought Him before the high priest for interrogation. When He had been questioned, the soldiers beat Him and mocked Him. The next morning they took Him to be judged in Pilate's court, where a large group of people had gathered outside. Among them, those who had praised Jesus as King now rejected Him and demanded that He be sentenced to death. When Pilate had conceded to their demands, the soldiers led Jesus away to be beaten once again. They placed a robe around His shoulders and a crown of thorns upon His head, mocking and striking Him. Then they led Him through the streets to be crucified. Nailed to a cross for all to see, He became the ultimate Passover Lamb, sacrificed for the sins of the world. ***(music begins)*** In His final moments, He looked out at those responsible for His death and cried, "Father, forgive them for they do not understand what they do." Then once and for all time, He paid the penalty of death in full.

From *No Greater Sacrifice* (55/1138L)

Behold the Lamb!

Words by
Pamela Stewart

Music by
Larry Shackley

www.lorenz.com

10
a bat-tered Man is laid up-on a tree.
13
cresc.
mf
The ham-mer falls, the nails cry out that pierce His hands and feet.
cresc.
mf
cresc.
mf
16
mf
for they
He prays, "For-give them, Fa - ther,

19
do not un - der - stand."
They come to cru - ci - fy a
22
26
man,
but sac - ri - fice a Lamb.
poco rit.
Be - hold the
poco rit.
25
a tempo
Lamb!
Be - hold the sac - ri - fice,
the One who
a tempo

27
gives His life to set you free. Be - hold the
29
cresc.
f
dim.
Lamb! The sac - ri - fice is made, the ran - som
31
mf
has been paid, be - hold the Lamb!
dim.

27
34
p
He dies a - lone
p
37
up - on the cross; the Fa - ther turns a - way.
39
f
The sky be - comes
f

41
as black as night, the earth be - gins to quake.
43
mf
And cer - tain ones who
mf
mf
45
wit - ness it be - gin to un - der -

47
stand.
They came to cru - ci - fy a
49
28
man,
but sac - ri - ficed a Lamb.
51
poco rit.
a tempo
Be - hold the Lamb!
Be - hold the
3
poco rit.
a tempo
8vb

53
sac - ri - fice, the One who gives His life to set you
55
cresc.
free. Be - hold the Lamb! The sac - ri -
cresc.
cresc.
29
57
f
dim.
mf
fice is made, the ran - som has been paid, be - hold the
f
dim.
mf
be - hold the
f
dim.
mf

59
Lamb!
Lamb! There was no oth - er sac - ri - fice,
61
no oth - er to a - tone.
63
mf cresc.
30
None oth - er than the pure and spot - less Lamb of God a -
cresc.
cresc.

65
molto rit.
lone!
Be - hold the
molto rit.
67
a tempo
Lamb!
Be - hold the sac - ri - fice, the One who
a tempo
69
gives His life to set you free.
Be - hold the

71
Lamb! The sac - ri - fice is made, the ran - som has been paid,
74
be - hold the Lamb! Be - hold the
mf
mf
mf
poco rit.
77
Lamb, be - hold the Lamb!
mp
mp
poco rit.
mp
p
p
p

Narrator: In the darkness that engulfed the afternoon sky, the earth shook and groaned. It was as if creation itself were overwhelmed with grief. Many of the bystanders fled, perhaps fearing God's wrath. Others were unable to move, rooted to the ground that still held the cross firmly in place. As they looked upon the face of the One they had betrayed, they realized, too late, the gravity of what they had done. Surely this was the Son of God. The Savior long-awaited by generations had been rejected and shamed, scorned and beaten, then crucified by the very ones He came to save. ***(music begins)*** Like those who stood before the bruised and battered Man on the cross, we too must realize: He came to save us. He came to save us all. And together, we can only bow our heads and say, "Hallelujah! What a Savior!"

From *Behold the Lamb!* (55/1175L)

Hallelujah! What a Savior!

Words by
Philip P. Bliss

Arranged by **Molly Ijames**
Tune: HALLELUJAH! WHAT A SAVIOR
by **Philip P. Bliss**

www.lorenz.com

13
SA
p mp
came for ru - ined sin - ners to re - claim! Hal - le-
TB
mp
God, who came
mp
poco rit.
a tempo
33
16
mf
lu - jah! What a Sav - ior!
mf
poco rit.
mf
a tempo
19
mp solemnly
Bear - ing shame and scoff - ing rude,
mp
mp

22
in my place con - demned He stood;
mf
sealed my par - don
mf
25
mf
34
poco rit.
Hal - le - lu - jah! What a Sav - ior!
with His blood:
Hal - le - lu - jah, Sav - ior!
poco rit.
28
a tempo
p
cresc. poco a poco
Lift - ed up, "It is fin - ished,"
p
cresc. poco a poco
Lift - ed up was He to die,
p a tempo
cresc. poco a poco

31

rit. **f** *a tempo*

was His cry; now in heav'n ex -

f

rit. **f** *a tempo*

8vb

34

ff *rit.*

alt - ed high: Hal-le - lu - jah! What a

ff

ff *rit.*

Sav - ior!

37

a tempo

Sav - ior, a Sav - ior!

Sav - ior!

Sav - ior, a Sav - ior!

a tempo

35
molto rit.
molto rit.
Broadly ♩= ca. 69
SA + opt. Cong.
f triumphantly
When He comes, our glo - rious King,
TB f
Broadly ♩= ca. 69
all His ran - somed home to bring,

45
then a - new this song we'll sing, Hal - le - lu - jah! What a
(8va)
36
48
end Cong.
Sav - ior!
Hal - le - lu - jah!
51
ff molto rit.
What a Sa - vior!
ff
ff molto rit.
8vb

Narrator: As evening approached, a man named Joseph asked for the body of Jesus and took it to his own new tomb. There he wrapped the body in linen and rolled a heavy stone to seal the entrance. Now the chief priests had heard Jesus say that He would be raised from the dead. They feared that the disciples might steal His body and claim that He had been resurrected. So at their urging, Pilate dispatched guards to secure the tomb.

Early on the morning after the Sabbath, Mary Magdalene went to the tomb along with two other women. There was a violent earthquake and an angel of the Lord came down, rolled back the stone from the tomb and sat upon it. The guards were so afraid that they fell to the ground like dead men. Then the angel said to the women, "Do not be afraid. I know you are looking for Jesus, who was crucified. He is not here. He has risen, just as He said. Go quickly now and tell the disciples." Racing back from the tomb, their feet could barely keep pace with their eagerness to share the news. Their once-heavy hearts were now light with joy! With every step, they must have repeated the words over and over again: "Jesus is risen! He is risen!" ***(music begins)***

Christ Is Risen! Alleluia!

Words and Music by **Mark Hayes**
Incorporating **MACCABEUS**
by **George Frideric Handel** (1685-1759)

37 **Moderately, with energy** ♩ = ca. 84

f

SA
3 *f*
All the world, re - joice! Peo - ple, lift your voice!

TB
f
All the world, re - joice! Peo - ple, lift your voice!

5
rit.
Christ is ris - en! Christ is ris - en! Al - le-

rit.

 JD

38
Faster ♩= ca. 88
ff
lu - ia!
Faster ♩= ca. 88
mf
f
mf
Grave, where is your vic - to-ry? Death, where is your
mf
mf
sting? Robed in light for all to see, be -

17
f
hold: the res - ur-rect - ed King! Christ is ris - en! Al - le -
20
lu - ia! He has won the vic - to - ry. With Cre -
23
a - tor God Al - might - y, Christ will reign e - ter - nal -

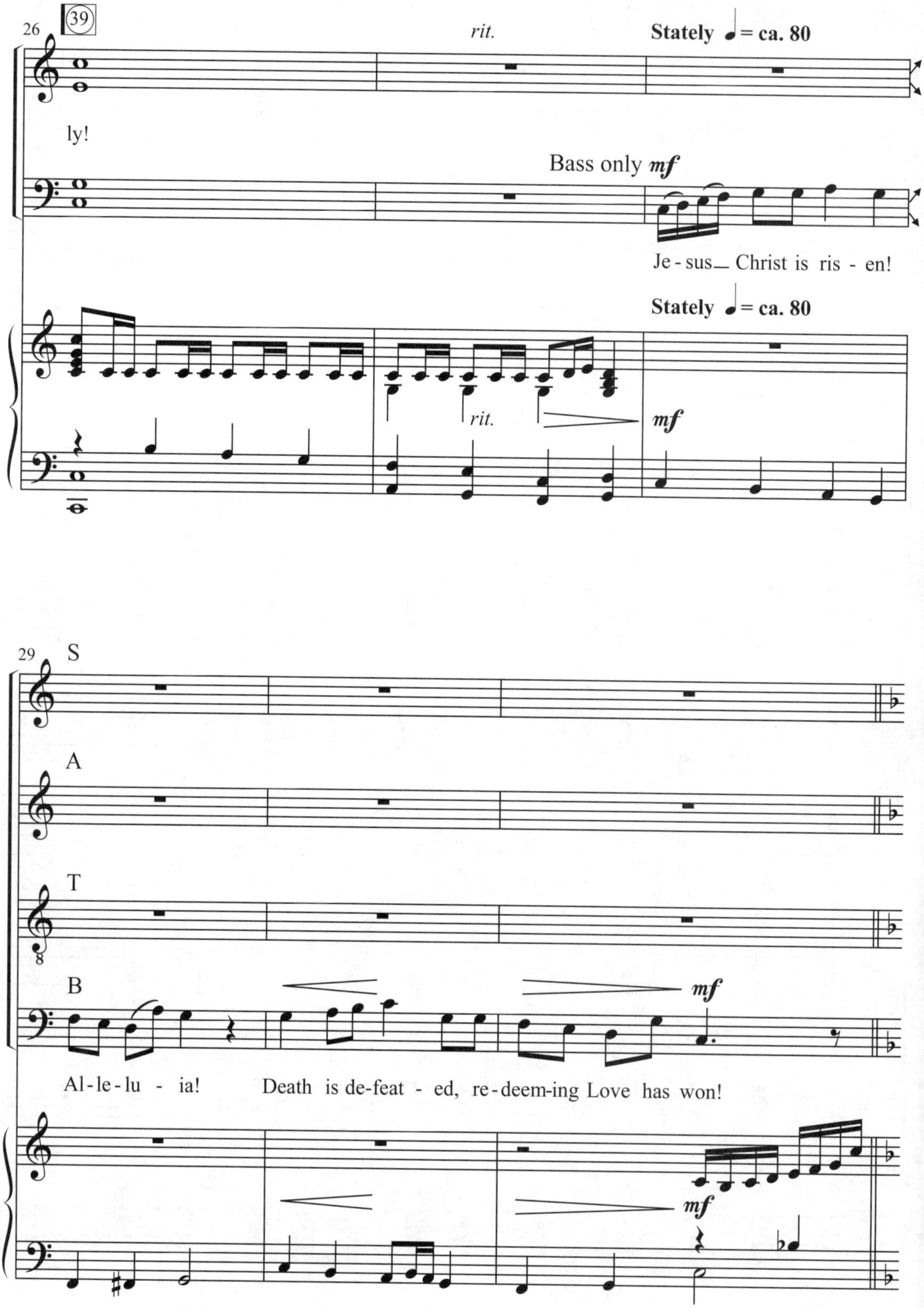

29
S
A
T
B
mf
Al - le - lu - ia! Death is de-feat - ed, re - deem-ing Love has won!
mf

32
mf
Je - sus — Christ is ris - en! Al - le - lu - ia!
Je - sus is ris - en! Al - le - lu, al - le - lu - ia!
34
40
mf
Death is de - feat - ed, re - deem - ing Love has won!
mf
Death is de - feat - ed, re - deem - ing Love has won!
mf

36
Je - sus Christ is ris - en! Al - le - lu - ia!
He is ris - en! Al - le - lu - ia!
Je - sus Christ is ris - en!
38
Death is de - feat - ed, re - deem-ing Love has won!
Death is de - feat - ed, re - deem - ing love has
Death is de - feat - ed, re - deem-ing Love has won!

40
f
Je - sus Christ is ris - en! Al - le - lu - ia!
He is ris - en! Praise be to God!
won! Al-le-lu - ia! Al - le - lu! Praise be to God!
Je - sus Christ is ris - en! Al - le - lu - ia!
42
Death is de - feat - ed, re - deem - ing Love has
Death is de - feat - ed, re - deem - ing Love has
Death is de - feat - ed, re - deem - ing Love has
Death is de - feat - ed, re - deem - ing Love has

44
SA
won!
TB
3
47
41
rit.
Majestically 𝅗𝅥 = ca. 63
♩ = 𝅗𝅥 f +opt. cong. on melody
Je - sus is
f
rit.
♩ = 𝅗𝅥 Majestically 𝅗𝅥 = ca. 63
50
ris - en! Death, where_ is your sting? Grave, where_ is your

54
mp
vic - t'ry? Hail the ris - en King!
Ban - ish shades of
mp
mp
58
sad - ness, shake off sor - row's gloom.
See, the Lord is
62
mf
ris - en, ris - en from the tomb.
f
Je - sus is
mf
f
3
mf
f

66

ris - en! Death, where_ is your sting? Grave, where is your_

42

rit.

Slower ♩ = **ca. 104**

Choir only

70

vic - t'ry?_ Hail the ris - en King! Je - sus_ Christ is_

Slower ♩ = **ca. 104**

rit.

74

ris - en! Hail Him,_ Christ the King!___

Je - sus_ Christ is

ff

f

8vb

78
Je - sus Christ is ris - en!
ris - en!
8vb
81
rit.
ff a tempo
Al - le - lu - ia!
ff
rit.
ff a tempo
(8vb)
84

Narrator: Christ is risen! He is risen and is now seated at the right hand of the Father. The scriptures tell us that one day, we will stand before the throne with the angels and the saints who have gone before us. There, unable to withhold our praise, every tongue will confess Jesus as Lord and Savior. Heaven will have but one song and all of creation will sing it: *Worthy, worthy is the Lamb. Worthy is the Lamb, who was slain, to receive power and wealth, wisdom and strength! Worthy is the Lamb to receive honor and glory and praise forever and ever! Amen, amen, and amen!* This shall be our song for all eternity! ***(music begins)***

From *Come, Touch the Robe* (55/1123L)

Worthy Is the Lamb

Based on **Revelation 5:11-13**

Words and Music by
Pepper Choplin

www.lorenz.com

8
Hosts.
Bless - ing and hon - or, glo - ry and pow - er to
mf
11
mf
Him who reigns up - on the throne.
44
13
f
Wor - thy is the Lamb that was slain to re - ceive

15
pow - er and rich - es and wis - dom and strength.
17
Wor - thy is the Lamb that was slain to re - ceive
19
45
hon - or and praise for ev - er - more.
for ev - er -

21
mf
I heard the voice of man - y an - gels, they were
mf
more.
mf
23
gath - ered 'round the throne.
25
mf
ten thou - sand times ten thou - sand, all the
mf
They were ten thou - sand times ten thou - sand, all the

27
46
cresc.
an - gels joined as one.
cresc.
cresc.
29
f
Wor - thy is the Lamb that was slain to re-ceive
f
f
8va
31
pow - er and rich - es and wis - dom and strength.

33
Wor - thy is the Lamb that was slain to re - ceive
35
hon - or and praise for ev - er - more. Bring Him
47
37
rit.
hon - or and praise for ev - er - more.
rit.

A few sopranos
39
a tempo
Wor - thy is the Lamb that was slain to re - ceive
SA
a tempo
I heard the voice of man - y an - gels, they were
TB
Clothed in right - eous - ness, robed in glo - ry,
a tempo
41
pow - er and rich - es and wis - dom and strength.
gath - ered 'round the throne.
ho - ly is the Lord of Hosts.

43
Wor - thy is the Lamb that was slain to re - ceive
They were ten thou - sand times ten thou - sand, all the
Bless - ing and hon - or, glo - ry and pow - er to
45
48
hon - or and praise for ev - er - more.
an - gels joined as one.
Him who reigns up - on the throne.

47
Wor - thy is the Lamb that was slain to re - ceive
49
pow - er and rich - es and wis - dom and strength.
51
Wor - thy is the Lamb that was slain to re - ceive

53
49
hon - or and praise for ev - er - more!
55
mf
A - men,
a -
mf
A - men,
mf
58
men,
a -
a - men,

60

men, a - men, a - men, a -

a - men, a - men, a -

63

cresc. *f*

men, a - men, a -

cresc. *f*

men, a - men, a - men,

cresc.

f

66

cresc.

- men, a - men, a -

cresc.

a - men, a -

cresc.

69

poco rit.

50

ff *a tempo*

men, a - men!

ff

men, a - men!

poco rit.

ff *a tempo*

71

rit. ***f***

A - men,

f

f *rit.*

73

cresc. e rit.

ff

a - men, a - men!

cresc.

ff

a - men, a - men, a - men!

ff

cresc. e rit.